# Benjamin *and the* Box

## ALAN BAKER

In this series:
Benjamin and the Box, Benjamin's Book, Benjamin's Portrait

HAPPY CAT BOOKS

Published by Happy Cat Books Ltd, Bradfield, Essex CO11 2UT, UK

This edition published 2004
1 3 5 7 9 10 8 6 4 2

Text and Illustrations copyright © Alan Baker 1977, 2004
The moral right of the author/illustrator has been asserted
All rights reserved

A CIP catalogue record for this book is available from the British Library

ISBN 1 903285 76 3

Printed in China

Happy Cat Books

Hmm, what's this?

A box!
I wonder how you open it?

Soon find out.
One twist of the screwdriver and. . .

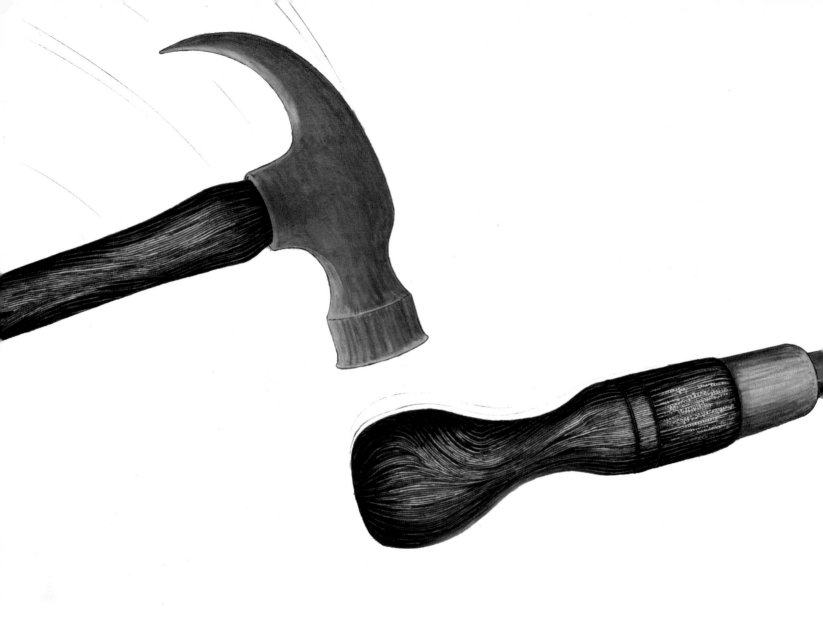

Oh well, this hammer should do the trick.

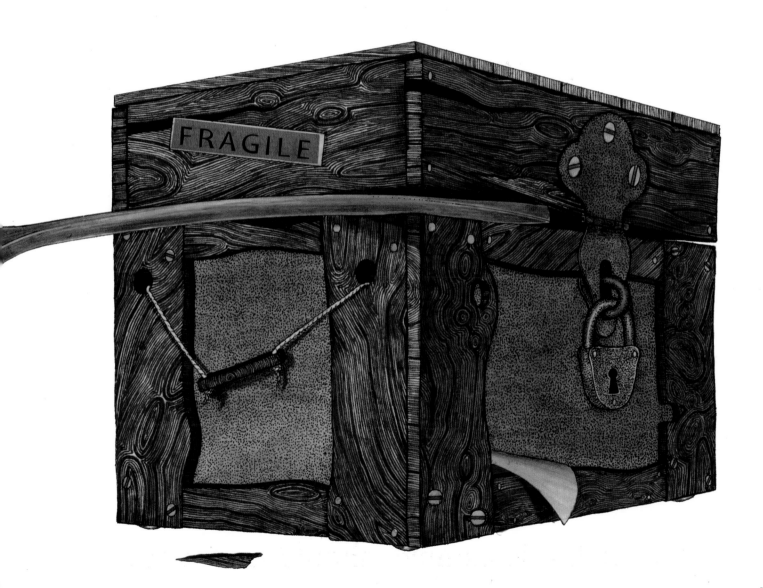

Not quite.
Push the screwdriver
in a bit further.
That's better.

Now the
hammer again. . .
BANG! BANG!

. . . Let's try something a little more subtle.

# Hey Presto!
Benjamin Hamster springs into action.

Abracadabra!

# Open box!

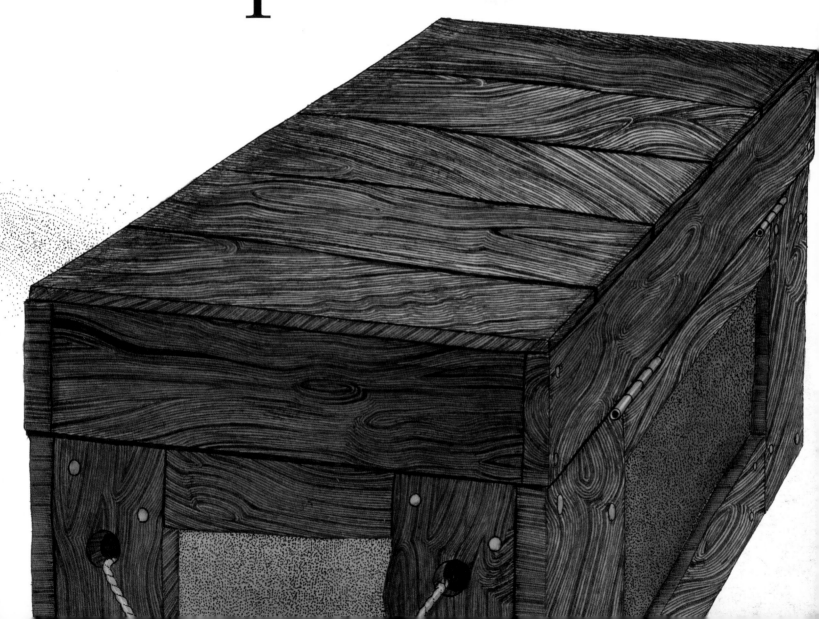

Hmm, I never did believe in magic.

What's this? A padlock.
How silly of me not to have seen that before.

Soon have this off.

# Oh dear,

I've set the box alight.

Water,
quick!

Whoosh!

Time for some brute force.

# Hey! What's going on?